TIME OUT OF MIND

Laurie Block is a poet, playwright and storyteller. He was born in Winnipeg and now lives in Brandon, Manitoba. His previous work includes a chapbook of poetry, *Governing Bodies*, and a bilingual collection of poems, *Foreign Graces/Bendiciones Ajenas*, based on his experiences in South America. He is also the author of a full-length play, *The Tomato King*, produced by Theatre Projects of Manitoba in 1997, and a short piece, Pop! His short story, While the Librarian Sleeps, won the 2003 *Prairie Fire* fiction contest and, most recently, The National Magazine Award Gold Medal for fiction.

Time Out of Mind

Laurie Block

OOLICHAN BOOKS
LANTZVILLE, BRITISH COLUMBIA, CANADA
2006

Library and Archives Canada Cataloguing in Publication

Block, Laurie, 1949-
Time out of mind / Laurie Block.

Poems.
ISBN 0-88982-225-5

I. Title.
PS8553.L557T54 2006   C811'.54   C2006-900511-7

We gratefully acknowledge the support of the Canada Council for the Arts for our publishing program.

Grateful acknowledgement is also made to the BC Arts Council for their financial support.

We acknowledge the financial support of the Government of Canada through the Book Publishing Industry Development Program for our publishing activities.

Published by
Oolichan Books
P.O. Box 10, Lantzville
British Columbia, Canada
V0R 2H0

Printed in Canada

for Johanna

૭૦

. . . all stories are like those about the creation
of the universe—no one was there, no one
witnessed anything, yet everyone knows
what happened.

—Jose Saramago, *Blindness*

Acknowledgments

ॐ

Some of these poems have appeared previously in *Prairie Fire, TickleAce, Writing Home, CV2* and *More Power To You*. Grateful acknowledgement to the Manitoba Arts Council for their generous support and the Manitoba Writer's Guild for time and space at the retreat beside the big lake.

A debt beyond words to Colin Smith for the support, encouragement and rigorous editing; to Shari and Susan Johnston of Manitoba Artist for Healthcare for the opportunity to learn the difference between healing and cure; to George Payerle for the wit and wisdom; at last and always to Johanna Leseho who teaches me time and again how to live, love and write with conviction, consciousness and courage.

❧

We do not have to improve ourselves; we only have to let go of what blocks our hearts.

—Jack Kornfield

Contents

৽

Coming to my Senses

Foreword: The Note

My friend Gary says it's time to write The Note. In a cursive hand, shaky or resolute, on fine onionskin that will not flinch when it is folded, again and again until it is only a fraction of its full compass. A text of a delicate gravity, sleeping in the nether reaches of my wallet as unobtrusively as a condom. The Note, without signature or date, that reads: *If you've forgotten why you wrote this, then it's time to jump off the bridge.*

Gary and I were caring for our poor, dear, demented mothers. Translucent bags of soft tissue and desiccated affection that we filled by spooning mush into their open mouths. We hated what they were doing to us; how their affliction had finally trumped us into caring for them; into negotiations with their lawyers and accountants; into end-of-life directives and weekly visits among madwomen inching their way into oblivion. We hated them for a silence in which we lived on and they forgot to die, irretrievably lost in a fog so thick and impenetrable that death could not find them. Near the end we were nothing to them, except perhaps the smell of tobacco, a dollop of ice cream, a kiss on the cheek. Our difficulty was of a different order. Try as we might we could not forget them.

We managed their affairs and made decisions to the best of our abilities. We had power of attorney, drove late model vehicles with power everything and, between us, could muster a pathetically random assortment of power tools. Dustbusters and drills that whined at our touch. But beneath all the accessories we had no power to let go or turn our backs, we had no good death to offer. We were, in our helplessness, not so far removed from them. Except for The Note. Which I've not quite gotten beyond conceptualizing, while Gary, who runs a daycare, is up to his knees in poop and rebellion. The Note is our default position, a passport beyond the shadow land. The Note will absolve and cleanse us. The Note will set us free. Or perhaps this is the delusion of a middle-aged man. If it's there in black and white, it can't be too threatening; if I authorize it myself, it won't hurt that much.

This is going to make me look bad but I'll say it just the same. I wanted my mother dead, departed, gone to her reward. It was impossible for anyone who knew her to get the point of her continued existence. It wasn't about her anyway. It was for me. I wanted her more out of my life than hers and so I asked for her death on a daily basis; prayed, not for the release of her soul, but of my obligation. If I'd had the guts I would have helped her out myself.

Characteristic of dementia, long ago my mother began to misplace words, to sift and search her mind and, when she couldn't find them, to substitute generic catch-alls like *whosits* and *whatchamacalit* for the names and faces and everyday objects that were slipping through the holes in her brain. I watched the gradual disintegration of language and took notes with a mixture of helplessness and fascination, as if I were a voyeur, a bystander at a particularly gruesome traffic accident; repelled, ashamed but at the same time aroused by a need to witness the carnage; the shattered glass, twisted metal and bodies under blankets by the side of the road. She was a passenger, trapped inside an inarticulate terror while everything, the scream, the impact, the insult to flesh and bone happened in silence and slow motion. For a time the words continued spilling out of her mouth like blood from her injured brain; like beads from a broken necklace rolling beyond recall or recognition; a stew of personal pronouns, indefinite articles, prepositions and possessives divorced from reference, object and precedent. *I gave him one of those and one of these and it went over there, up and around and the next thing I knew, POW, right in the kisser.*

Words stalked her like unhoused spirits, dispossessed wraiths passing back and forth through the walls of her unconscious and deep into dream time. She began to speak in what I chose to believe was metaphor, an attempt to bridge the intolerable vacuum of the present, to reach forward and across to the far shore where the future had long since disappeared and the past had preceded her. Call it poetry or simply a random and accidental series of neural impulses, she was still capable of feeding me truths embedded like raisins in the raw dough of her confusion:

This is the palace of nothing.
Ella quenched me.
To be living is to be crying.
Two black houses, that's it.
You mean you'll wear my pants?

I remember the last coherent words she spoke. I was reading her the newspaper, *Dear Abby*, from the foot of the bed when she lifted her head, and, arching her eyebrows as if she was still capable of pouring the vinegar into the milk and sucking on irony, said: *you know, I used to be quite fond of you.* This was before the vacant stare, the wheelchair, the diaper and the bib. In the end she forgot how to walk and took to her bed. Flat on her back in the nursing home, her pale translucent skin (of which she'd been inordinately proud), stretched over her cheekbones and deep into the last century. She looked like *Little Big Man*, the oldest living Cowboy-slash-Indian-slash-Jew in the world, a refugee from history. Her eyes stayed closed, her hands were useless claws and, though she was under sedation, she slapped them for hours against her thigh and on the armrest of the wheelchair. Maybe it was irritation or maybe she was sending a message, tapping out a plea for release, a desperate code that I couldn't crack.

In reality, when Death finally dropped in, it wasn't as lyrical or instructive as I'd hoped. She suffered a minor stroke and stopped eating. The alternative was a feeding tube and an IV drip for liquids. I nixed this and stood around her bed for nine days while her heart beat faster and faster and her breath grew shallow and the sheet over her chest moved up and down, up and down until it subsided into stillness. Toward the end she could not swallow and a nurse came on the hour to squeeze a few drops of water into her mouth *for comfort,* her body a sponge that filled and emptied until the heart could hold no more. In the end she starved to death and I allowed it. Then I applied for a writer's grant to support the graphic aspect of my grief. Good ol' Mom.

In my proposal I wrote how, here in the Canadian flatlands, much of our poetics is rooted in disorientation, displacement and disequilibrium, the friction between what happens outside the skin and what goes on inside. This presupposes intense yet intermittent connections to those moments when we have our feet firmly on the ground, where we walk steady and know where we're going. It's my belief that we value the mind as more enduring and connected to assumptions about identity than our bodies; that somehow we'll be in control until the very end, hands on the wheel, ten o'clock, two o'clock. If not, what is there that endures? Is the Self first a face or a soul; a composite of sensorial inputs and neural receptors, or is there an inner other life, an integration of spirit with a Prime Cause? Those of us who work what we are into words, entertain the hope of an afterlife in text. Like dry bones rising, I wanted these poems to wrestle with the nature, change and decay of consciousness through the culture-specific lens of illness, age and death and then, to speculate about the experience of those who, by reason of disability, stand outside this help and hope, whose perceptual field is closing fast. I wanted to address questions in which the fundamental integrity of memory is implicit. To name a few:

What if you don't remember (or can't know) what you want? How can you either register or resist desire?

What is the measure for loss?

If you can't recognize who is close at hand and who is long-gone, how can you (re)enter relationship or absence? If you can't discern boundaries then how can you cross them?

What if you lose the horizon? Without the straight and level, how can you tell what is imminent from what is out of reach? How do you locate yourself, read the map of the here and now when your compass is out of whack?

What if there is no shared context, field of experience or

common path to travel? How can language and relationship persist when every experience is personal? How can the heart go on without the "other"?

Until my mother died, my take on Memory and its loss was mired in the abstract. To give it flesh I did the only thing I could, I wrote out a progressive record of her dementia; an autopsy of consciousness and its many faces—cognition and emotion, memory, belief. While the body is bound to place and time, the story of a mind is more fluid and mutable, following the shape of the vessel.

As an early childhood teacher I observed the mind's unfolding from birth, swinging from the theoretical monkey bars of Jean Piaget. Now I saw development in reverse. As prime care-coordinator for my mother for over ten years I studied consciousness under the gun of pathology. In her spiral back to infancy my mother lost the gift of keeping the world alive in the absence of evidence. Once a thing is out of sight it never was or would be. She lost control, sucked and whimpered like an infant, her repertoire of responses (I'm convinced her hold on life itself) no longer directed by will but reflexive. If abstract thought is, in part, the liberation of being from the whirlwind of the particular, than dementia stands the process on its poor bruised head. My mother experienced the world from the inside out so that everything was personal and invasive. She became a membrane which the world she once inhabited passed through. The spoon, the elevator, a bird, me, we all came and went with the breakfast tray, disconnected and beyond her reach.

This leads to the end of the biological and poetic line. Death I imagine is the hammer or the pillow, the ultimate contextualization. Like comedy, it's a matter of timing. As long as you keep your hands to yourself and meet it head-on, Death does occasionally beat the alternative. All the blessings and apologies and restorations we are able to leave behind us hold the possibilities of peace. The solace available in a closing line and a last look back; the chance to set things right and take your children off the hook, closing the door softly as you make your exit. In poetry I aimed to draw a map of dementia; its mechanics, physics, music, and geography: the stages of descent, the loss of grip and balance. I'd hoped for a belly response, vertigo. What I ended up with was, I fear, nightshade, nausea, a poisoned and lugubrious text which ripped me apart in the making and near killed me to read aloud.

Fortunately, at this point, life changed. I grew older, fell in love and began to understand for myself how to live with consciousness and write with courage and compassion. I began to ask for what I wanted and developed an expectation of joy, a disposition to gratitude. And what to make of love? Do memory and the organs of ecstasy work in harness? Are cognition and perception necessary and sufficient to nourish and sustain our apprehension of the Other? Is love a cultural or an ambient condition, a state as elemental as water and light; a primal field that surrounds and penetrates both consciousness and the senses, simultaneously inside and out? That's how this book, *Time Out of Mind*, took a sharp turn to the left and became something else, as we all must do.

Lights Out

It's just life. Or what happens after.
The residue. The footprints.
That's why they call it pathology.

—Robert Clark, *Mr. White's Confession*

The Presentation of Self
for George Amabile

In transit or waiting your turn
at customs, wherever the heart has gone
out of the sun, drinking a Corona
under the tricolour of the post office
you wait for word from home, a slice
of lime winking through ice
at mounted statues and women emerging
from morning mass, the plaza on its knees
roped off and empty after prayers
except for the excavation and cathedral door
black eyes and a beggar's open hand.

You are precious metal, you are rock
and for you the traffic divides, winding
across the belly and the breasts of old Mexico
its stained hills, the double aureola
of sunset and blood. Spiced skin,
smells of chocolate and smoke
loop your ruined afternoon, the light
glances off your watch and whistles
for the waiter, promising pure gold.
The turquoise serpent
you bought in the market uncoils
from your neck and sinks
its fangs into your thigh.
This is where the gods are buried
this is where to dig.

Next Year Country
for Roz Friesen

Saskatchewan 1934.
What a sorry place
to be born, a difficult time
to be slapped into life
spilling her first words
over grim stubble. Today
the cancer's got her

and we call it by name
as if history and disease
were our prodigal children
so wilful and out of control
we fear them and love them
in secret. The Great Depression

followed The First War discretely
as if they were biblical sisters with a gift
for prophecy when in God's truth it's always
happening, famine and war inside
the parched heart and unforgiving
grid of barbed wire and bank interest
the section lines of seasonal hunger.
A time to kill and a time to die.

Bad luck stretched forever down
miles of wind-strummed fenceposts
nothing alive on either side
endless dirt roads with nowhere
to go except to town or down
a dark well, a dry hard kernel of hope.

The earth itself lay broken, starved
and cracked, a promise everlasting
dry on the stalk. There were thistles
in the pasture and flowers
in the sloughs, there were mouths
to feed and grown men weeping
in barns, wet cheeks against the mare's
nervous flank, toes on the trigger
wives and children listening
for the hollow report of the fool
who bought the farm.

Saved in a sense by the second
war and I suppose we had the jews
and gypsies and faggots to thank
though in those parts who'd even smelled
a jew, peacetime being an outlandish claim
on the garden when all the engines
of cash and credit, tears and blood
watered the overworked earth.

Her bed a lot like the vacant prairie
cover stretched thin
against hospital chill
sounds of mortality drifting over her body
footsteps and hushed alarms
the dry intimate rustle of those writing
lists and folding their possessions
before the final winnowing.

Her mother once gave her a wooden suitcase
painted red. She dragged it down
the lane into a golden afternoon
it must have been fall, though the wheat
had forgotten, the trees understood
when she took their leaves and laid them inside

as if they were gifts from God, newborns
at the breast or pages from the Book of Love
to get her through the worst, the world
of doctors and needles and pain in the night.

When she closes her eyes she flies
home to reclaim the soil
of her childhood and finds it
beautiful still, alive in the dust
and smoke of memory, the sun ripening
to red over the ghosts of trees she knew
the sunken homesteads and helplessness
of men scratching at the horizon
bewildered.

Poison & Riot

Shy in the presence of beauty
unsure of strength and confused
by both the visible and unseen

you run through old conversations
about the value of life, self-worth
and enterprise, what is permitted

and what remains taboo, whether to decorate
the walls or crush the world outside
the skull where the garden goes on

pushing through cracked earth and time
worn symbols of obedience and rebellion
(women and men, flowers and weeds). The crop

you harvest raises troubling questions
about which side of the rainbow you slid down
your craving for strong flavours and heavy scents

for sex to force the fruit. Make no mistake
whatever your persuasion the green wheel turns
and this world wakes to the chromatic voice

of want, to unequivocal musk and the blossom's
ingenious tongue filling the morning's throat.
Pick me pick me and your heart hums

images of attraction and surrender
reach through the sky. You are loved
you are lonely, the planets continue their dance.

It's the law. Pale shoots lift their heads from dreams
of earth, painted fingernails slice the dark
membrane between the eye and the beloved

but nothing stops at the skin. Sensation crosses
the line between the flesh and all you were told
has neither limit nor name. There is nothing else

but to work the soil of ecstasy and remembrance
no other remedy but to express your life
in print or in poison, in riot and symphony.

II

Like love it appears to happen overnight
the wild iris pitching a purple proposition
to the green and sluggish pond. From a hole

in the sky the eagle takes note, dropping
a tailfeather on the burning rock. Bang—
it's that sudden, the shift from rumour

to movement and on into image. A rise
in temperature, molecules accelerating
then it's over, the reflection that opened

your eye and filled it with light and shadow
the illusion of a silver bowl superimposed
on a still blue lake. In fact your senses are

already shrinking back to normal, the body's
sac of stammering assertion. One sure thing:
without this transformation you're as good

as dead. Die any way but only once, grieved
and swallowed. Yesterday you were a fish
in your mama's moonstruck belly

today you're growing teeth and darkness
comes on kindly. Soon you'll be a thumb-
print, in the dust (naturally), the scrawl

of glaciers and mountains scraping by
a memento of the past, your parting kiss
moi on the pale fevered cheek of the earth

Time Out of Mind

Sunrise, sunset drift earthward
like ash from orthodox rooftops
shacks where a fiddler frets the season
like a show tune baring his head

to the unholy city. Man proposes
God disposes and on the seventh day
the boots come off. Unrepentant
the old man beats time with a crippled foot

and homemade wine. All he needs is sugar
and fruit gone bad, a deck of cards
a lucky hand. She is an instrument
on his knee, a handwashed pinafore

and a brand new bow, she's the string
section as he sings, wheezing in and out
his old-country accordion breathes
the lyrics against her new breasts' tremolo

her high-pitched double shame
and insufficient legs. Protesting inside
the bell of her sister's hand-me-down skirt
she descends the wooden staircase

slumped against a familiar shoulder
poverty with its unwelcome smell, sour
apples, garlic, a hunk of rye in her pocket.
She is nobody's violin

but if she were she would stop that song
yank his tongue from her mouth and drag it
through vacant lots and waist-high weeds.
With one pure high note she would shatter

the bones of the hand that holds her
like a schoolyard fence wherever she goes
the boys run wild, shadows squirming
they whistle through blades of grass

pipe her name through dirty fingers smelling
rhubarb, sunlight, soap. One day they strip
the secrets from her lips and fling them
to the wind. She bends to them like wildflowers

presses them to her chest as if they were babies
she could hold against her skin, root them
back in her belly, safe from the slash
of the sinking sun and gravel underfoot

ice wagon and ragman's sorry nag
street breaking into song, a wedding party
turns the corner, waves of laughter and gabardine
dance in darkness disappear into joy.

Later the bed shakes as a train rips through
her sleep she's dreaming she's a wheel
and can endure almost anything except
this midnight run, the shuttle and grunt

of cold blue steel the inconsolable cry
of the engine rolling through, empty.

Slap

Even before I arrive on the ward and check in
with the nurse I know it's my mother by the sound
a relentless hammering as she slaps her knees
and the arms of her wheelchair punctuate
the lunatic corridor, a long day closing
with a dull thud and an open hand.

This is no case of nerves, the drumming
of a mind on edge or absent
as it taps a table or the crystal face
of a watch, fingers feeling their way
along the smooth hard surface of an agenda
toward cancelled appointments and imminent events.

Nor is it holy vacancy, autistic hands
rearranging the sacred furniture and music
of a deep deep world while waiting
for the call. There are no visible signs
of grace as she bangs against the mystery
of matter and the limits of medicine

only the wreckage of what she used to be
a vacant lot littered with orphaned shoes
and unwanted metal, the broken springs
of thought and language where all she knows is
to kick it into life, shake the machinery
until it starts to run like it did.

Remembering the Bird

I now direct your thoughts outside
the nursing home where the window
in its frame becomes a cage
the bird attacks like a knife
passing across the old woman's eye
a brilliant slash laying bare
the clouds the sun hurtful

another day without a lid
spills its deep blue ink
over the ungovernable wind
and the awful gossip it spreads
undoing all her good deeds, the strings
of coloured facts she weaves
into her nest, the leaves' agitation
weak tea and telephone lines
humming a song to her golden years
when there was still a chance
of rain and the wide open appetite
of the young to fill, how she took the sun
for an egg and brooded over it
til it cracked

                    Coming to earth
the shovel-tailed grackle redeems itself
with every drink. In spite of the gravel
and grating voice there is music
grace in the gutter as it tips its beak
with every swallow its iridescent head
bobs in reverence to the heavens
stitching the sky to its reflection
elegant, blue

Forgive this bird
the season's mindless chatter, tuned
to the north a fierce heart beats
two hundred times a minute until
it bursts. Behind the glass winter perches
on human shoulders slowly filling the day
with personal effects as if it were a purse
snapped shut on the last pitiful tokens
of belonging: scented tissue and rings
of obsolete keys, lists of names and numbers
long out of service, a story about a saint
and the sacrifices she made. A diamond
she lost down the sink, babies
that ruined her figure, her image
in the riddle of soap as she locks the door
for the last time on the wing and gone
without a note

Pureé (with eyes shut tight)

Toothless now she cleans her plate
with her eyes closed against the shapeless
grey pudding of meatloaf and candied yam
yesterday's stew and the mystery of a mind
swallowed whole. What used to be solid
dissolves, the bewildering menu of her senses
reduced to one bland fact, no salt
to trouble the invalid tongue.

Dessert agrees with her. With a pinch of sugar and drugs
crushed in strawberry jam she no longer tears the skin
from her fingers. Ravenous and eager as a baby
bird she wolfs down the animal and vegetable kingdom
a procession of plates and names and faces that appear
out of nowhere, spin and blink like dying stars
across the thin red sky behind her eyelids
where a double moon predicts the coming storm.

And shall we give thanks for this delicacy, her grace
in going slowly? Must we bow our heads to boiled chicken
with potatoes, consommé, weak tea?
She dips her fingers in the soup and her face sinks
to the table as if the heart had failed, fallen
into the reflection that fills her bowl
where, if she looked, she might read the future
what was spilt and what remains within reach.

The poor soul drops an earring in the apple sauce
and chews on her loss riding a plastic spoon
through memory's kitchen, the sound of breakfast
burning, the smell of ruined sleep and voices
hissing, AM radio, intestinal feedback, stains
singing out from a lavender blouse
steam from a kettle boiling dry.

Senile Dementia

I want to know what happens next but I don't know how.
—Mary, May 21/99

First your hands fumble after midnight through the anarchy
of the cutlery drawer as if you left the light out there in the rain
of your second best silver one thing cool and familiar to touch fits
your hand and your feet believe what has always been there waiting
behind your eyes the urge to turn back the way they show you
a door and you slip the deadbolt, prowl the dark dreaming
streets in your nightdress. What happens next mother you lose
your nametag and forget the tune drift beyond music
the thin voice of an old bag of bones crooning to herself
they can all go to Hell.

What happens next your body sinks slowly and you're watching
yourself in a dance that dream of falling the fear that roots you
to this chair beneath the clock measuring urine and disinfectant
with your chin against your chest mouth open the long hallway
of wheelchairs and hampers charged with soiled laundry
a beggar's parade to the lounge where others wait their turn
to make birthday cards and refrigerator cookies
that room with a southern exposure television
and a caged bird the morning sun.

What happens next is your choice. If you persist in your refusal
to eat they may open you up really a small incision
under the ribs a clear plastic tube you can't reach and if you do
without the necessary force there are clips and anchors and collars
to stop that and if you do manage they'll only replace it
according to written instructions they'll bind your hands
in clumsy quilted mitts until you lose the map of blue veins
the vagabond itch misplaced under your heart.
This is how you'll take your three squares.

32

What happens next old girl your skin grows thinner
than memory turns you inside out membrane like a tongue
or the inner lining of your mouth and sex you'll register
every shadow tuned like daytime television to the restless
steps that assume a critical importance the arrival
of the lunch cart disappearance of an ordinary bird
across a window the compelling red EXIT and pungent smell
of old women and their sorrows moves you more
than your own flesh and blood calling out *mama*
mama wondering why with the whole world begging
that sainted lady holds her peace and your womb
doesn't dare contradict and give you the news.

What happens next is the bars go up and the circle closes
around your bed though you can't see beyond the bright familiar
teeth you can smell the perfume of grief the unintelligible
amazement of those who bring you sweets who keep your name
and papers and the watch imagining your last breath.

What happens next is you're cold and a face appears
to turn up the heat and draw a blanket your chin rides
your chest up and down the gentle slopes
that are the heart's achievement
into a golden valley the theatre of childhood
where you are today's matinee and poorer
by a dime the others shuffle down the aisle and out
onto the avenue half blind and relieved
in the end they can not follow.
Darkness is your ticket.

What happens next is it makes no difference
whether you remember what the trees have forgotten
what waters run from and rock accepts
at last you reach a clearing where the earth turns
merciful and opens, where you empty and what used to be
so hard turns to sand.

33

X-Ray

The poor creature extends an arm
blocking out the sun with her thumb
she presses down until the skin bursts
memory melting into a darkness
soft as wax. The attendant takes silence
for *yes* applying lotion in diminishing circles
the smell of fallen fruit and flowers
that open only in the dead of night.

She finds her voice in doorways
in the open mouth of the elevator she cries out
like a tenant testing the air for vacancy
a passenger who's missed her stop.
Who took my goddam baby?
Gimme back the sun, crazy talk held high
against her heart like a lead apron
over the blinding thought of death.
I'm the brakeman I'm her motor rolling
shush into a room with a mural, blue skies
buffalo and blackbirds that tell her nothing
about her upcoming appointment.

                    This is only a test:
they reach deep inside where the sacred
breath shakes the banner of self
as it travels like barium under her skin.
The doctor's bent on knowing, hopes
to throw some light on her disease
yet nothing grabs his eye but the old fracture
a thin bright bone breaching the surface.

                           It's not critical
only a reminder: what are the chances of making it
to the end without losing a wheel, without the morning
shift rifling through the ribs that bracket sleep
and what's a body to do anchored to a chair
between peagreen walls and ammonia, stainless
steel and porridge rolling down a hallway
for its own good. Today's a hot bowl
of good thick soup, tomorrow's that missing spoon
an empty hoop she can't quite get her hands
around what she always knew to be true.

Myopia

This is the needle
this is the eye, rich
with error and presumption
a lonely jeweller cutting diamonds
out of the small hours before sunrise
correcting their imperfections. Is it a leaf
or a bird frozen on that branch?
Is it measurement or a word
left wanting, art or nature
old friends approaching from the other side?

That woman you come upon, bent
over to your left on a smudge of concrete
that woman who cannot see
you taking her as a gift
in the grey time after waking might be real
a runner addressing her shoes
tightens the laces that connect her
to the path, dedicated to each pair of eyes.

The first is for her children, the one shrugging off
the comforter, the other buried deep
in dreams. Next comes the man with one leg
hooked over her and there's no avoiding
this escape, the sweat she'll break into, the river
running over the bone between her breasts, salty
taste in her mouth, faint irritation
of last night's love. The last tug is for her alone
the steps she's taken, the drumming she'll make
straight through the heart and dust
of a restless city, leaving you flatfooted
thick-fingered and fumbling with the loops
of a vision, how this woman who is not in fact

a fire plug but alive and unstoppable as the sun
clears the trees and distance ignites her
she's off and you'll never catch up
to her disillusion.

What Time is it Mister Wolf?

Suppertime and all her little lambs scatter
across the playground the wolf hot
on their heels. Where are her children

now she's in danger of outliving
their bruised knees, their joyous terror
coming home late after dark? She is *it*

alone in a field where shadows choose sides
lining up against the chainlink fence
between the seagreen grass and sealed windows

of the nursing home. The game is over
when day breaks against the bars
of her bed and she wakes with her teeth safe

in a teacup, passed over yet again
an old woman's shoes trick her
into rising like dough, the bones of her

pumped up overnight fill her dress
asleep in the arms of a folding chair
love's labour undone.

Morning opens the door and shakes her
by the shoulders the night nurse relieved
groans from the toilet as she cracks

her eyes fully dressed folded and obsolete
as the Sunday paper a blur of tilted faces
and voices at full volume broadcast vitamins

juice and a promise *dear,* today something special
cinnamon toast and sunshine but mum's the word
they're on the prowl, sniffing the air

for the runaway bride, an old woman in pink
slippers and a straw hat with a mind of its own
sewn into the lining. Imagine if you can the worst

that's how the mending gets done around here
under the furniture of yesterday's fable an imp
no bigger than your mother's silver thimble

sours the milk, steals the baby and leaves her
nursing a nightmare. The fur-faced runt chews
a nipple and makes free with her good name

dragging her purse in the dirt. When she lifts
her skirt they are nowhere to be found
her rosy complexion, the flowers she pressed as a girl

First Door on the Left

Your new address on mercy street
round the clock care doctors on call
but without memory you are a tenant

of the open window the contents
of your chair. Your day jumps out
of the dark like a neon sign a brief

flash of colour with cold fire inside.
The living come unbidden the dead fill
your brain's single bed with long hours

accusing faces and persistent clumsy hints
as if elbow grease is all that separates your soul
from the next world that if only you worked hard

enough you'd find your way across. Running
your finger along the edge of a mystery
dealing in dust you descend the staircase

walk yesterday's derelict halls stopping leaks
with chewing gum and virtue you throw yourself
headfirst into motherhood as if we were babies again

or hardwood floors in need of a polish you love us
to pieces discard nothing save what you can
the house bursts with insecurity and junk

bits of wool and bobby pins batteries and string.
The world comes at you damaged.
There's no telling what you'll need to repair.

After the War

she picks a path, steps over the ruined streets and gaping
vacancies of the North End avoiding the insults
of the pavement and dirty words on the walls
the park still haunted with immigrants, men
out of work and homemade wine exchange castles
for queens but where is Selkirk Avenue?
Where is the room, and her mother
worrying with a cold bowl of soup?

Windows boarded up but she doesn't need to look inside
to see how it's changed for the worse. Alarms at all hours
sirens threading through backyard talk and no-one looks up.
Accident my ass, someone's responsible for this intersection
with flashing lights and a bent tricycle, the one-eyed
van spinning its wheels while an ambulance idles, ready
for injury. It comes with the territory, dirt yards tattooed
with broken bottles, disposable diapers, needles, glad
bags, a child-sized violin and down in the cellar
you can be sure the dogs have had their day.

It's a long way back between the coming and going
between the standing up and falling down it's a thin
white hope, groping for the years she misplaced
the bridge she used to cross to the library
where she borrowed the gift of words.
She's getting colder and no-one speaks
that language around here. The jews are long
gone, not a soul is left to tell her
how things stand or where to catch the bus.

Crossing

Machines built to sunder and machines built to join
straps and clasps, buttons and buckles, ceremonies
of connection and release that make it easy to love
lose and get over it. But in the time before maps
were drawn and lines laid down and the gates
of the kingdom descended for good, a man might step
from solid ground for food or safety or simply to hold
up to the light what he'd seen only in the shadow world
of dreams, pale fire and a seductive voice urging
him across on a vine or fallen tree, in a leap

or in loving. The first bridge was no accident
but the blueprint of a mind reaching out
of the body to close the distance that stops it
touching what it wants in the world.
Consciousness is more than an accessory
of reason and sensation, a live wire in the harness
of couplings and circuitry that make him human.
Thoughts come to him in waves, an exchange
between bodies, intimate yet nameless as water
inevitable as breath they propel him beyond
his groundless fear to a place where the will is purified
where he can lay down his struggle to be good

to do God. In the moment of birth he crosses a span
from a world without form to the quick and plastic
present where he begins by howling for a balance
he's born to overthrow. Like a Russian doll each day
holds the next and deep inside contains
his future, lifetimes of labour and delight,
layers of science and poetry. The material world is not
the only bridge nor the easiest. Even if he could fly
he'd follow the hard road staggering under the burden

of words, looking for a line to hold onto
an image to ease him into holy ground

Lights Out

Your absence has grown
to the size of a grapefruit
floating beneath my skin
irreversible, neither self nor
other but an organ or a thought
without a home, a question
that won't fit and can never be
answered or forgiven.

Don't you go dying on me
again, bending one morning
to tie a shoelace or to open
your book, you lost your place
falling into silence, a hand
at my elbow, a voice
turning and returning.
What did you mean to say?

That this room will be a comfort
that the earth will continue
to amaze, whether or not
you are here cool and familiar
to the touch, darkness will contain
the loss, something to bump into
press against like a wall
or a dream you insist on
passing through, these words

only a membrane, a story
I can neither finish nor put down
stumbling between the beginning
and the end, feeling for the door.

We Chemists of Grief

Real memory does not induce regret.

—John Raulston Saul, *Voltaire's Bastards*

The Goods

The world continues to worry no matter
what you sell or give away, the material universe
perseveres. Possessions outlive attachment
utility, breath. This explains the bargain
tables stacked with electric knives and swag
lamps, birdcages and books, the stranger
in your mirror and children serving tea
on heirloom silver, this accounts for the poor
who go begging for work in your discarded suits.

Close up the house, seal the windows
cover everything in sheets
as if you've only gone for a season—
soon you'll be skipping
up the stairs to inhabit the laughter
in the kitchen and the smell
of your favourite chair, the memory
of your body at peace. It's difficult
to relinquish that dream
slipping into the familiar
picking up your story
exactly where you left off.

This passion for detail surprises you.
Who had time to think about dust?
There were jobs back then and babies
to care for, damp clothes and the whole
blessed universe crying for attention.
There were daily obligations and bombs
falling on distant cities, death in dark skin
to consider and so you marched
signed letters, manned the soup kitchens

did a world of good but who had the nerve
to go all the way, to chuck the book club
and the fitted sheets and commit to that other
life, the aluminum trailer on the edge
of the desert, the hopeless litter of drowned kittens
and unpublished poetry when deep down you knew
sooner or later someone would up and die
and there you'd be, on your way home, dragging
something with a handle, a suitcase or beat-up satchel.
There's a season for coming clean and it isn't always spring.

Fadeaway Jump
   for Carl Ridd (1929-2003)

Picture a classroom, the pulpit or the cold grey streets
of this city as his arena, a ball and a court
without judgement. Given his natural gifts
good hands and vertical extension, lift
and trajectory, whatever the score
the game offered a season of second chances
to learn, to become himself playing his way
into redemption. Repentance meant turning around
and shooting for three from the inside, sin
meant missing the mark and he was an arrow

in front of a class, Carl was often beside himself
with delight, that body in His image like a brush
across the blackboard made perfect sense: God,
play, art and justice coming alive in relationship.
Talk flew. Language was more than a leg up
on a half-hearted ladder, it was our responsibility
to unfold our minds and extend our bodies, to stumble
out of our hearts and into the world. *Ex stasis*
he'd launch himself skyward and land, light on his feet,
knees apart and slightly bent to absorb the impact of the Word.

It was not the education I'd been groomed for.
What did I want with *goyishe* nonsense like basketball
and existentialism? I was bright and bound for glory, sailing
my desk into the real world of privilege and reward
where it still counts as weakness to love too much
and admit to doubt. What good would it do me
to discern the voices of the Holy Ones, to see the world
reflected in the cold clear depth of a poem? Remember Oedipus
of the easy answers and swollen feet, the hard road
he hobbled into prophecy, blind on three legs.

Now the match is over and the bell is rung
waves of worded sound spread from the still point
of this day as we try to keep him here
with stories. In this way we warm ourselves
remembering how he moved his body
through the wounds of knowledge and the cracks
in language toward beauty and justice
how we are all free to carry what we love and believe
and imagine into the world of action, to hold out
our hearts with a graceful strength.

Big Picture

Outside my window I see a great letting go
over the vertical shell of the city
over walls and doors and cluttered concrete
shelves, lives stacked in layers, story
after hard-luck story stirring in the first light
where the trees spend their savings
and the profligate sun risks
a year's gold in one inspired burst
the season slowly undressing
returns the glory it borrowed from the earth.

Morning traffic idles, running
on-the-spot, winded and frozen
in motion as if chronic greed
and acceptable levels of pain
were only an excuse, an exercise to refurbish
a blown-out heart and keep the blood
pumping through the hidden chambers
of belts and pulleys where it's work
enough to feed the moving staircase
endure the sick buildings and fifteen
minute breaks, dreaming of down time.

In the corner of an eye a single spruce
survives the foetid breath of the great grinding
machine, branches unfold over a bench
where a lone figure slips into its sex
crossing a leg or dropping her shoulders and refusing
to be swallowed by the insatiable bus
as it lurches toward terminus, on schedule
engorged. She will not cling to one shape
or fasten on a single destination. Is it an illness
to remember the days of gathering

leaves and tunnelling through the ruins
when she told time by the light and tumbled
into the magic kingdom, home free?

As children we knew how to fall and live
with bruises, now we study stillness
save our bones. The passions of the material
world pass around us and leave us cold
as if we were rocks in the middle
of a relentless river or hearts
loving nothing and helpless
inside the monster. Free
if we allow the changeable light
to find what was lost
to reveal what lies buried alive
within our bodies. This time
this place of beauty, the year
with its tangible finale
when the heart is held aloft by grace
and, by will, disclosed. It is our winter
and our choice to walk out
into a cold pure night
to let go of the light
we absorb in our loving.

Do-it-yourself

the sun came with the Avon Lady
at ground level sweet bells
perfume from the waist down
her legs scissored the sidewalk
the sky was a ribbon
between her knees a procession
of shadows the blue rumour
from which he fell

thirteen winters in his basement
working on the life of a saint
with powertools and instructions
and voices drilling him
with the law on his side
and low monthly payments
it's a handyman's special
it's the ideal place to sleep

in his dreams he is the egg
within an egg he is the perfect tenant
invisible absent in his dreams
the rays of the sun pass through him

Hospital Blues

Still life but muted and subdued
off-white and empty as an easy chair
the grey city and river rising below

a bright room on Palliative Care
where a singer takes requests
stirring slippered feet

into memories of movement
and youth, the insistent beat
that once drove them to dance, to know

their bodies beautiful
to hold one another close
and breathe urgent words

against skin, against the cold
dull weight of afternoons exposed
and in distress. Because she's dying

Gloria lets fly singing as if she were the last bird
waiting for that old midnight train
to rumble by her window

all feathers and clatter and hurt
uncoupled at the edge of town
on a night *too blue to cry*

with the smell of smoke and shooting stars
sparks curling from childhood
fires, the flavour of raspberries and stolen

cream under her tongue, a song
resplendent as ribbons
unwinds down the corridor

and it's almost enough
to wake the dead
that twang as a promise snaps

the high note when the screen door slams
and a heart grows cold
in a room at the end of the hall

The Lame

The lame insert themselves behind doors
like brochures from a funeral home
folded with care they are the souls
of discretion   envelop you with whispers
ruin your meal with a smile

The lame will drive you crazy
with their lives   the hours humming
at the mirror   lighting up in church
folding laundry after sex
you want to fix them
or give them away to a good cause

The lame do not blame God
or take offence   they tell stories
transparent as the wings of insects
flimsy as rice paper   their history
of tissue and mishap that is not myth
they have no gift for magic
or instruction   the men rattle on
whistling at machinery   the women are experts
in surgery and bad luck

They work door-to-door   the lame
take the census enumerate read meters
in your absence they leave polite notes
shot with symmetry   breasts and teeth and testicles
ovaries and toes   even numbers
thrill them their lips tingle
to name their obsessions
organ transplants a second tongue

Don't despise them for their innocence
when they accept collect calls
from old flames   how their nerve ends
trick the skin where it's been stitched
and phantom limbs make love
follow their tentative hearts
you'll come to the ocean
the end of solid ground
you'll measure each footfall

 Have mercy on the lame
for those who live with amputation
pray for paradise like no-one else
they are true believers
in grace and resurrection and the day
that dry bones rise
they'll cast aside their crutches
and take the silver staircase
two at a time   they'll leap into ecstasy
in the arms of a perfect partner
they will dance the night away

The Consolation of Small Engines

uncomfortable in black dress shoes
my neighbour hung over
the fence between us
orphaned hands awkward suit
rare white shirt   lights
a smoke   it's all for the best

> *the pain is done yah she rests*
> *with her hand right here where it hurt*
> *yah nights were hard   on the needle*
> *every four hours but no comfort yah*
> *nobody to care for her breathing*
> *thin eyes going grey by the time*
> *I got home she quit*
> *checked my watch*
> *twelve-twenty or thereabouts*

call it going home
after years of making soup it's something
to consider as you turn to dinner
washing up in the summer kitchen
with a bar of sunlight
she would approve

he mourns the farm the yard
contains his loss weeds and lumber
ruts that fill in the spring
with rainbows of gasoline ducks
under her clothesline Monday's wash
wrung out by hand
what good is the wind to him

starts his truck and a tractor
idles   the ford wants a sparkplug
his hands know the gap to jump
the question of timing before it starts
humming the requiem of hard work
internal combustion   he spits
wipes his hands on a rag
of flowers cut from her summer dress
wreaths of blue exhaust
the steady consolation of his engines
if they stop
this is something he can fix

Going out

like a candle or a bedside lamp it's convenient to see
death as a construct, a device that regulates time
like a clock or the all-night mystery channel

on slash off you get the forecast you get lights
flashing in your face and a door closes
the elevator inches down a sunless shaft

that's how we've rigged things with wire and switches
it's our culture and we don't want to know
what holds it together, who's asleep at the wheel

the years roll on and over, ladders puncture the sky
so why all this fuss, dying is neither punishment
nor possession, only the end of one relationship

the beginning of the next, of being only outside
looking in. Remember that feeling when you dream
your death take it as a touch from an old friend

one who comes in time, who's travelled far to see you
across. Your body is the vessel, the freight's on board
and death is that inside passage. Like love

you can never be sure where you stand.
At the appointed hour death slips into the mouth
of the harbour rising like saltwater to help you

with your luggage. *It's a mistake* you protest
you're all booked up and expecting someone else
you disguise your pleasure as an accident

thought as dust and your body an old leather bag
forgotten on shore but nothing sails without you.
Death follows its timetable with the patience of a cat

coiling around the ankles of those who drown
on dry land, who pussyfoot along the fence
as if they were only waiting for a fair breeze

as if they already knew how to fall. *Red sky at morning
sailor take warning.* Death has its dark side, duct tape
and exacto knife, a record long as your arm.

Un/Afraid

I

I don't trust those graveyard men
with their shovels and hidden picks
their teeth all smudged with tobacco
and tongues rimed with hunger. I am leary
of true believers, salesmen walking the golden mile
in knee-length boots and leather indifference
opinions and pharmaceuticals slung like trophies
from their belts. I'm afraid of the line
drawn in the sand, of border guards
with their trick questions and windowless rooms
the anonymous kiss of folding metal chairs.
I tremble in the presence of uniforms and the hands
of clinicians, freeze in the glare of surgery.
I prefer ghosts over doctors, sunrise to gravity.
I'd rather kill time in the mind
of a memorable November than be swallowed
by a professional smile imagining cancer
in clean white clothes. I've been a glutton
for punishment and a fool for love
but I'm having second thoughts, not
making it, how satisfaction boils
down to a matter of
timing, success slash
comedy it's my funeral.

II

I am not afraid of the water
nor the wind that breathes spirits
from the east and knowing waves
of oxygen across my wakeful skin

my love rises early, alone and inevitable
as the sun, thorough as the mist off the lake
she lifts the hem of the horizon and shakes it
rearranging the tangible blue sheets, rocking

my one-man craft. Naked from the waist up
I am a hero in the eye of my canoe, half-man
half-vessel for that astonished god
whose story does not divide this world

from the next or tear the body from the soul
but holds the mirror, reminding me how I swam
into life all beautiful and crying out, that my flesh
was conceived not as a garment but a miracle

stitched to this image. Fear is the mark of separation
from this narrative, the deep dark bruise of a heart
without a voice. Picture the morning after the storm
one last self-conscious leaf on the bent and troubled tree

of endless winter where there is consolation in nothing
but the skin. There I was drowning inside my loneliness
a swimmer against impossible distance. The harder I pulled
at the horizon, the more it shrank from my touch

as I struggled I sank only deeper in personal waters
until love lifted me from the rocks and restored me
gasping to my soul. Now I reach across the blue divide
rejoicing the air in my lungs and the island I am

riding the generous belly of ocean, the full skirts
of the midnight sky where I hold earth's eye
like an heirloom ring on velvet. Though we are small
and far apart faithfully we shine, the stars and I

still cast our nets across burning waters where the moon
gives birth to itself a second time. As for this world
of animal beauty, listen for the loon embracing the end
of the day. Between rock and water its sweet and grievous song

sustains all mortal swimmers with a few notes
to cling to in the crossing, an unfinished anthem
for every creature that dives through the depths
for all those who sing out in darkness.

Curtain Call

I

Nights alive and full
of oxygen, sleepless figures
drift beyond the point
where the mind stops dealing
in what's available second hand
in all there remains to catalogue
in the first person
possessive. There's a limit
to thinking with these fingers
turning ideas into property.

This little light of mine
fades into fact the minute I make it
my business, ransacking
nature and dividing the spoils:
birthmarks and a slice of lime
mahogany sailboats at anchor
in dark waters, a leaf-shaped bruise
on a woman's throat.
The intimate stream of images
passing through my bedroom
dissolves in the morning, incomplete
except for my unclothed body and sense
of loss, beyond which I dare not go.

II

Last night I dreamt Spain, seedless
red grapes and children immaculate
in white, Catholic streets alive
with a passion for bulls, blood
and sacrifice, a world redeemed
by faith and innocent lips
framed in a moustache of milk
on the road to communion.

To compare a dream to a curtain
rings false as a string
of costume jewellery
in the clasp of those who stagger
from one world to the next.
To come down on the safe side say
this is not a metaphor
say dreams *are* curtains
hanging there like sexual fruit
burgundy shadows pleated
with the promise of syrup. Pretend
every dream is your theatre
your story about to unfold
in the holy hush of the stars
in the plush tumult of light
tumbling over your shoulder.

Right Time, Right Place

one day you step out and apart
from fallen leaves and the sage
stubborn silver and ambiguous
green, the rocks and hills
have always been there
on the lip of a vanished ocean
in the cry of distant birds
in the drought of now or never, in the wind
that brings winter and the thick sadness
of words, people who fill your hours
with desire and disillusion, how they disappear
forever running off because something happens
inside like a nail driven deep, like a window
without glass and who can tell, who can

resist self pity when no one loves you
you think maybe you're nothing
maybe they can smell it on you
despair and the liquor of need and away
they go leaping like the deer balancing
their hunger on legs brown and slender
as the dying grass, on their genius of being
here and gone enchanted by your eye
the way a jackrabbit freezes and a poem
shows its face and it's just the same
as loving and it's all you ever want.

Narcisse

If it's all in the execution, the play unfolding
according to plan then the poet's in a league
of his own. He can imagine himself
tackling the dazzling blond defences
of his dental hygienist but football is war
bruisers in uniform punch air crack ribs
collapse against each other swaggering
mountainous but not so brilliant as rock.

No one left standing. Outside of slow death
and shrivelled testicles from where I sit
there's no trophy in it no beauty
until a wide out name of Narcisse
abandons the huddle and goes deep
leaping out of inglorious shoes he undresses
the air with a twitch of his hips shaking
loose from the desperate clutch and grab.

The field falls at his feet like clothes
on the bedroom floor and hey
who showed him those midnight moves
that sweet love muscle how he spends his self
easy, long gone like last week's paycheck
king of soft hands and slow mo.

Man he was god that sunny afternoon
his number on the big screen high above
the trap block and collision of flesh
on flesh he was stitches on the ball
and a perfect spiral in the superblue sky
he was lightning on tiptoe down a thin white line
with the crowd's wordless roar and delirium
on his face it's a healing when you hurt
and Monday morning hits you blind side.

A Bowlful
for Roz Friesen

It begins, the filling up and remembering, with visiting hour
an old woman rising unexpected from the thick mud of forgetting

to the surface of the moment, her mother-in-law coming back
to deliver one last gift: *I'm going to die. Now you'll have to learn*

to live without me. It begins one more time in the way all stories
cry out for a second chance, with a girl at a table and a bowl

of homemade pudding. Chocolate. A man's face offered
to a window that opens into the larger world where facts

happen: parades take place and voices break against the glass
receding in waves as children cross streets and objects drift

dreamlike from one hand or pocket to another. Night follows
without fail and the pudding, still hot, grows even sweeter under

a thick kiss of whipped cream that will inevitably turn sour.
The child knows this, the table shimmers with transformation

with the possibility of every new sensation moving her beyond
appearances, the surface of her world shrinking as it cools

but the fire remaining, hidden and close to her heart
as if she had plucked it from the heavens, set it to her lips

and a thousand bubbles appeared, like craters on a chocolate moon
the skin of the pudding shaped by primal breath. She has not yet learned

this is caused by the weather of the kitchen, how steam cools
against the cold belly of cream and falls like rain over small appetites.

This is the way hot food calls out to the spoon, how sugar invites
a mouth to approach. She is satisfied with this parable of God's

69

miraculous recipe, male and female, pleasure and science swimming
together in one bowl. Her world changes, day by day she grows

speaks and imagines. Temperatures rise and fall, molecules collide
the beauty of the planet beckons. This morning the man hones his razor

to a fine edge, testing it on a hair before he addresses his blue
shadow. An old song about blackbirds through the open window

white sheets and shirts hanging in the sun, a mountain of responsibility
and lather thick as whipped cream on the loving bowl of his face.

Papa, why are you shaving? He pauses (I get the idea he usually
takes his time, as comfortable with the sharp edge of silence

as he is with the razor) and turns his full attention to the child
and her question. *I'm going to a funeral,* his blue eyes speak

from the mirror as they did at birth. *Papa, how long does it take to go
up to Heaven?* Along the corridor between this world and the next

the man measures distance and time knowing his child will envelop them
in his words and carry it through her life. *Three days.* Such a long wait

for what you only know in dreams, such an inconceivable journey
for a body stepping through childhood's door into the vast room

of being and doing. And so little time to prepare.
Once she believed she was capable of anything, mending the planet

with a few adjustments, a loving stitch here, a deft patch there.
Now it is enough to breathe, here in the passage between two doorways

Roz cradling her life and leaving it so softly that she can wait for the pudding
to cool and stop for her father to answer, fully restored in her consciousness

70

in the words and music rising above her bed. Nothing is spilled
nothing wasted. From the clean white page of this unanticipated day

her hands dance through air and, dipping deep into the sweetness
of the only world she knows, she holds out her bowl for more.

She Rises Without Fear
for Aileen Olsen

The Almighty is with me and if He is with me who can be against me?

The souls of all animals are visible just beneath
the skin, braided in breath and muscle, in the flare
of their nostrils as they inhale the night before bending
to drink from hidden pools. St Francis found it
easier to follow their sacred music than the desperate
human dance, how they step to the tune with more grace
and less effort than we educated dispensers of guesses
we chemists of grief on two legs. So pardon me for turning
my back on the busy hospital hallways, gleaming machinery
and mountains of medications to follow a story
into the forest. It's about the hoofbeats of deer and death
and an old woman's memories moving her toward a healing.

Fear finds no home in her, hovering for a moment
like the shadow of a small hunted creature, a chill
passing, the smoky signals of the spirit world
have her full attention. Even when she needed no-one
to clothe and clean her, even when she was young
and carried an apronful of worries she embraced
the miracles that appeared on her lawn. White-tailed
deer approaching from the four directions emerge
from the groves of remembrance. As she steps out
her kitchen door singing *the red red robin* they come
to her most sensibly enchanted and alert on legs delicate
and temporal as willow buds in spring and whispers
in the evening. *Sophie* she calls every deer *Sophie*
for it is an ancient voice and a timeless knowing
that schools them to lay their heads in her lap.

After the music she feeds them. Bread and apples
corn and cranberries but it's not the need
that brings them round it's the drumming
of the herd on a familiar path, the reassuring
rhythmic patter of belonging in a benevolent
universe, the scent of safety and health on her
that draws them out of the darkening forest
into a clearing of unrehearsed reverence
and undemanding eyes.

There's love there
a love she believes you can't compare.
With people it's different, there's love muddied
with fear and anger, streaked with words
and bodies shrinking away from the demands
of being and the deep hollow hunger of the soul.
And so we come to harm while neighbours complain
about the noise or pretend they know nothing.
She's no saint, they make her so angry sometimes
she'd like to kick'em clear to kingdom come but
she's not built that way so instead she learns to shoot
prayers, line them up in her trusty sights, squeeze
the trigger and *hallelujah* their goose is cooked
without blood or sulphur she asks God to soften
their flinty hearts and help them arrive
at a hands-on understanding of hard times
and what the other fella goes through.

For death is a river running beneath the floor
of every apartment. It's the escape clause
in the mortgage, an act of God or caprice
of nature. You can get mad or get even, cry out
for compensation or swallow your pride but it's best
to leave the table, open the door and walk free

because it isn't what you eat, it's what's eating you
and there's cancer abounding. She is not afraid
though there's a hole in her throat where her words
mix with the air, though she's drowning on dry land
she believes in rescue, that she'll rise again
and float toward the other shore on waves of glory.

So why not welcome it as you draw near, why flinch
from the fingers of practical nurses and today's notion
of a cure, long needles and strong medicine
the thousand and one indignities, offending organs
that leak, drip and dry up, the love offerings
deposited in stainless steel basins. One day
we'll all get old, sick or broken and isn't it good
there's more than disappointment and the fugitive
breath. Death is no hunter nor are we prey.
If there is a quarry let it be the consolation
of troubled hearts, the comfort available
in the fallen stones of the temple, in the beautiful
ruins and pure intention of God's law.

Though death is far more tangible (and negotiable)
than the great abstractions, what brings it a bad name
isn't the cause but the effect, how no one is certain
where it all ends, in nothing or wonder, rapture
or fire, the grim expectation of a treacherous path
up an impossible slope or a descent from the summit
hellbent for leather and out of control. For her
it is only a stopping at the edge of the great woods
and the deer, stepping softly to the lyrics of a popular song.

Thirst

Toward the end she cannot swallow
every hour the nurse comes to squeeze
a few drops of water into her mouth

for comfort her body a sponge
that will fill and empty
until the heart can hold no more

and her tongue goes still. Unconscious
she lies and lives on a bed of silence
deaf to her name and the weather outside

poor bird a cloud obscures the mirror
the feather barely stirs as her gown rises
falls rises falls to mimic breath

and her skin its unearthly transparency
as if it were an open window
where she might float away

but for the weight of clean sheets
and two cool fingers taking her pulse
a palm light on her cheek sufficient

to tether her to this tenement of flesh.
Who will pay the penny and do
what must be done? Shake the holy dust

of remembrance over the bones
that gifted you with life
over every name misplaced

and tenderness forgotten over all
our numbered days as they fill the glass
touch our lips and spill over

Natural Law

A confession, that summer of separation
when my loneliness towered above me
like a red pine blocking out the sun
when gulls circled and plunged and never stopped

crying, I once scratched out my fears
on birchbark stripped from the living
tree. A script as sharp as a knife, as deep
as the desolation written in my blood.

I couldn't imagine life without my mother.
Nobody else came close, the camp filling
with the songs of children busy carving
character and diamond willow walking sticks.

No one else entered the dark tangled wood
where I'd etched my name in living tissue.
I knew true love called for sacrifice
and organic matter, pitted primitive forces

against skin and bone and nimble wits.
Words come easy and trees plentiful
but mother's a dying breed and the body
remembers. Take this down: I believe

the natural world scripture enough
that spirits walk about embodied in trees
clothed in clear water, invested in rock.
Held against the sun they tell the story

of miracles that escape the ordinary eye,
this beauty I can't contain in the crossing
from birth to death: the golden tongued fern
curling as winter approaches, a spider

playing on that cool branch between
appetite and snow, whiskeyjack jamming
for a handout on hunger's growling sax.
This is where I come in, tapping my toe

to a minor theme, banging out words.
Believe me, I am no better than the dirt
under my fingernails, brothers and sisters
I am the thief who got off lightly

picked the messiah's pocket and melted
into the crowd, strapping on the sacred
like a stolen watch and searching the walls
for a crack to hide my conscience

a secret passage back into childhood's forest
where the season scrolls open
and the planet lifts her face as if she were a bride
rising in bluegreen communion

to receive the available light like a kiss
like poetry half-remembered or a song
broadcast across fire and flood
without consideration for which god

is working overtime or who is consumed
in the flames. This much I've learnt
about wood and consummation. I serve the gods best
when I want the sun and burn for love

when it's real I can catch it
like the rain on my vagabond tongue
when it's real I can hold it
in the hoop of my thirsty heart.

Mrs. Nielsen's Dance

While the orchestra still plays
I can stay here no longer
inert in this wheelchair
counting out my days
in intervals of meals and medication
while doctors bend and bow
and the nurses step so softly
to the hospital's helpless hush.

I will rise up now and skip
light across the morning
slip beyond the grasp
and machinery of old age
the steady drip of sugars
from wheeled and metal trees
how all my precious moments pass
in silver shoes and aliceblue gown
buttoned or not I shall waltz
lively between those double doors

with boys and paper flowers
hanging heavily against the walls
my heart will move to a lofty beat
young ladies coming
through the rye and the world
I once knew shines
across gymnasium floors
the years gliding by
heel and toe side by side

in the schottische and minuet and my skirts
atwirl with a shy tremour
one damp hand on the small
of my back yes actually touching
rough wool and music and oh
my the smell of soap and clean
white cotton boys and
brilliantine and afterwards

you ask me *Did I dance?*
why I wore out shoe leather
kicking up my heels
in The Rose Garden and The Cave
spinning through the dawn
of a lost generation
with girl singers swing
orchestras and bottles
under the table in brown paper bags
bandstands in the park
bicycles and bonfires
beside the river and before the War
the boys all men and pinned
inside suits and boutonnières.

Remember I was born for this
midnight and roses
silk and cologne my father
singing in a dream
ties ribbons in my hair
night falls in ringlets
gold on the pillow my pride
my joy I remember the day
of surrender in three small steps

across the threshold the barber's
quick scissors and red chair
turning turning in the mirror
when the music stopped
I cried at the loss.

Coming To My Senses

The different names for the soul,
among nearly all peoples, are just
so many breath variations and
onomatopoeic expressions of
breathing.

—Charles Nadier, *Dictionnaire
Raissoné des Onomatopées Francaises*

Delicious

A ten-year-old partially eaten grilled cheese sandwich sold for US$28,000 on eBay yesterday. The seller claimed its toasted white bread bore an image of the Virgin Mary.
The National Post, Tuesday, November 23, 2004

Who made this world
so hot and hungry
for salvation that we swallow
each heavenly bite, oh mystery
divine, oh angels descending
to earth, saints with breasts
bandaged flat and hearts
baked to perfection
in the penitential oven of prayer.

They rise golden and done
to a turn, Christ on a tortilla
His Mama on grilled cheese
Mother Theresa displaying herself
on a cinnamon roll in Bernstein's deli
believe-it-or-not. What the hell
was that succulent nun doing
impregnated with raisins in Nashville
of all places? How could she
flog herself on eBay for God's sake?

Which turns my thoughts to the other
ordinary women I know and cherish
all the friends and lovers, wives
and mothers, singers, healers
sisters and teachers whose sweet souls
don't need to be worshipped to reveal themselves
in the steaming kitchen of language
in the double-boiler of love.

Where is your single mother
on macaroni, your dyke
on camembert, the Avon Lady
in crème bruleé? Why not
a librarian or a tennis pro
a poet climbing
the circular staircase of sorrow
one step at a time
as all women do?

Skin Deep

look nothing is flat
fatman your waist band
buckles your button eyes
squint even the horizon swells
let it roll the blue appetite
beneath you bony prairie
conceives another day

take off your shoes fatman
and kiss the pink road
open your eyes
you've been this way before
reeling in confusion
on soft buddha toes
drop those empty clothes
forgive your belly
your beauty cries for light
your only hope is air and plenty of it

Button Button

who's got it, who wants to be
that child racing against time
to fasten self to circle
cause to effect

a small thing really to close
the fabric of personality
over hunger and quick feet
in darkness we are born

in death we whisper
for candles and words of closure
from love and from the living
we want transparency, a shining

to fly up and into
as if it were a prize
to hold fast to keep what's rare
and hidden safe in our grasp

a secret button to undo
the moon and the waters of night
bring down the river of dreams
and remembrance the stars

dropping like cold tears
even as the sun slides
its flat brass head
through the blue celestial frame

morning and the bright pavilions
where all children burn to know
and reach quick hands deep inside
the living heart of the lost kingdom

to solve the dark knot
of the senses and wake
the sleeping beauty bring her
back into the light

Out Loud
the second Johanna poem

I come to you barefoot and step tentatively
inside as if you were a hidden pool or wild
mountain creek, as if I didn't already know
your temperature and your depths.
This is not the time for islands, for waiting
on shore striking off the days
until rescue. Now is the moment of crossing
to reach into the horizon and touch the uncertain
line where sky meets ocean and the waves
lay the gift of their return at my feet
carry you away and bring you back
to teach me about rhythm.

Words are more than bubbles of sound
in the heart of a stormy sea
distance is not a problem of measurement
say this twice, *distance is not a problem*, loving
no solution but the medium in which we move
like dust in sunlight, that point off-shore
barely visible and just this side of the horizon
where we hold one another in suspension
and occupy the same body of water
the same thirsty skin. Your voice contains me
like salt in the sea, when you speak my name
I swim between your lips and stroke
for that holy ground where breath breaks
into music and speech, one pure exhalation
in the night, a platform for the spent
and desperate swimmer. *Window*

you call out and there I am leaning
into the unfenceable evening calm
field you whisper and I lie down
looking up through the smudge of cloud
the rumours of wind framing your face
in red clover and sage. I am listening
to your hair in my hands and words
like cool white stones follow the contours
of our bodies' conversation, this furrowed ecstasy
and humming procession of wing and tongue
the fallen seed opening into glory, diving
like me into green genesis to write
the first book, to tell the story of stories.

The Dive

High above the pool and hesitant
clinging to the high tower pink
and innocent toes curl like questions
toward the wound in shining waters
the slash along the surface
you'll repair with silver stitches.

This is the beginning of flight
when you leave your feet and wriggle
free and falling fill the air with illusion.
In your brief and brilliant descent
you are an arrow and a bolt of blue
Shantung silk your breath breaks
on entry into a perfect string of pearls.

Turtle Time

He wakes up alone and safe
inside the clamorous shell
a pilgrim in blood and bone
husband to science and nature
inside his fridge where by degrees
breakfast turns black and eggs
grow spiteful in the ruins
of marriage in the memory
of lettuce his spirit turtles.
What to do what to say?

Words endure but actions
hammer a conclusion
in softer elements he whistles
on his back under a machine
on his knees before a fantasy
loving maps and good strong rope
the straight line from the city
to the fallen temple
between all he spent and all he saved
wrestling with angels in two dimensions

In truth most seekers never find
what called out to them
from the other shore
they die alone at the foot
of the glass mountain or adrift
clinging to the craft
of their small beds and the company
of strangers as if they were holy
beads or a vessel bound for home
a lantern in the thunderclap
of voices *Who goes there?*

These whispers drive him
mad love love love, lubricant
divine till the end of time
exit. The soul depends on skin
like a gateway needs a fence
the way walls want windows
how in his prayers a man asks
god to stand between
what he wants and all he knows
the complicated smell of darkness
the persistent outcry of blood

Borne again to drape creation in the fabric
of imagination as if it were an island
or a medieval bridge beauty and decay
brush his eyelids like ribbons
bright on the limbs of a dying tree
like fingers reaching through the blue
prairie sky his eyes fixed
on the horizon his ears filled
with thunder and speculation
what will be no more and what is still
to come the smell of lilacs
and rain pressing against his lips
an open window in the summer
kitchen of carbon and desire

This must be dance
to shrug off the winter
of dark consideration
as if it were the robes
of an unjust angry god
to drift like a leaf or a hand
in cool water. This must be love

94

breathing where the animal still runs
three blackbirds and a fox
alert and certain in wild oats
and jimson follow his unconscious
gestures the shadows of tenderness
that slip through the three strand fence
fingertips on cheekbones on eyelids
and lips the sound of wet grass and the sun
coming up astonished the surprise
of being surprised yet again

The Turning

When it's abundantly clear you're in
free and deep and over
your head when the map opens
wide and whistles
when every purple mountain
and back alley anthem is easy
and all you never knew
about loving theory and practice
asks for you by name talks
you down and in and out
of lofty distress to a place
by the river where the wind
sings its intimate song against
your naked cheek and every
emergent tree and stone-broken
stream rises at your entrance
splashing stillness over desire
shadow in the sanctuary.

The earth will never be as patient
as it is today, stopping to teach you
constancy, to move in circles
through the dark hours.
Already the sun blushes
turning its face from midnight's
muddy fear to roll through the one
great circle that has no edge
enclosing all you want
or imagine you can now dive
blind into the moving centre.

Your body takes its time for once
trails unhurried shapes like beads
in deep water like wings
of memory and migration
you feel her fingers drumming
you home with the urgency
of summer and children
long past dark, the heart
of a small bird immortal
in her hands unfurls
the banner of natural music
a capella under the stars.

Home and Away

I'm learning to cross the water.
The years have taught me to trust
the current and the wind (when
they are right) to take me easy
over the lake, fingering the torn fabric
waves and the furled leaf
of a canoe, the needle
of a compass, my island
at two o'clock where I'll sleep
on earth rest my bones
against a tree.

It used to be work. As a young man
I heaved more weight and moved
faster, relied on forceful constructions
arm strength and heavier line
to anchor my obvious truths.
Pleasure was round
the bend, hunger at my back.
The horizon mouthed a tangle
of windblown prepositions
that fixed my place inside
the elemental question of who
I ached for and what I was
running from. How far
there was to travel between
what I knew and all I dreamed
of being.

Now the silken hollow of the tent fills
and billows with images
that arrive in darkness, a woman's
hands lifting with music, notes
in the margins of a book
clouds: a bird or a bear, bound
to the weather.

I find I'd rather touch than interpret, love
than collect the shapes that connect
the animal to the dream: open water
articulate rock, the paddle
that joins my arm to the river
this berry turning sweet
in my mouth.

Time Lapse

With winter still alive
and snow a layered veil
above the prairie's present
hunger and perennial thirst

the crocus digs itself out
of imagination and memory
spoons thin air balancing
the weightless delicacy

of the sun on yesterday's
green blade where a single bud
bleeds into tomorrow's purple
flower. Picture it shining

the chill subsides
the earth warms up
a handful of honey
bees in the heat of an ordinary day

this buzzing commotion
the demands of consciousness
holds an awkward camera
to the transparency of wings

a season's breathless metaphor
the call to blossom, to give
body to this earth
opening at your feet

This is for life
the first Johanna poem

I knew her, from our first encounter understood
this woman knows me in a way no one ever will
that through her love I was opening to images
I'd never allowed, shape-shifting quicksilver
goddess whose reflection I recognize
in coffee cups and ladders, in the melting
snow and exquisite riches she feeds me
sweet cream and honey on the rock, a box
of chocolates and that space she opens to me,
the place she sets at her table where I lay down
my deepest fear.

                          Now I travel light
and lord, I love this highway, this smooth road
unrolling in its own measurable course
back to my only room where it's clear
that broken yellow lines cannot diminish
her presence at my shoulder cupping the light
of return. Traffic overtakes me and the night
passes by without regret. I know my place
follow the signs with her memory on my fingers
I feel when to turn, how I'm moving
in the right direction and I'm not ashamed
of this uncomplicated devotion
my unadorned craft. This is not a map
an approximation of a journey with rest stops
along the freeway and hesitation
at the border. This is for life.

Now She Tells Me

According to official sources
that woman never did manage
to fix the world in seven days.
She only volunteered to do light
housekeeping and the decor
apply the finishing touches
one room at a time
making the rounds and righting
the wrongs of a previous day
she'd rearrange and put away
dusting off the dark trim and god
given air as it passed through
imperfect windows.

The night rolling through
histories handwritten
in the bluest ink available
recalled the first morning
of her waking when at long last
she realized how love is made
but light is born.

So *boom* she invented
incandescence smack dab
in the middle of a kiss that was more
than a chore but less than a miracle
he was bald she was willing
but ever so slightly
unimpressed when it slips
out her tongue and the words
she can't hold back or wrap herself
around the sorry sight.
You remind me of a light bulb

with an overbite. Here ends
the embrace and the man
justifiably freaked out
asks the inevitable: *What's*
a light bulb and *did I say*
something wrong?

As to the first heaven
only knows but I suppose
I can make it up as I go
along improvising she rolls
up the sleeves of her naked
imagination and plunges
her hands into the most brutal
and overlooked corners
of the kitchen and while glancing
over her shoulder adds
a pinch of unrequited salt:
It's not always about you buster.

More than a thing or two she's learnt
from fried onions and butter
milk and mystery
by trial and error she knows
there is no recipe for transformation
to change the world you got to trust
your instincts you got to wing it.

The first light bulb
she cobbles out of chocolate
expensive Belgian it only serves
to sweeten the night melting as it does
in her mouth. Next she banks on
tears which come easy and cheap and only

ruin the Persian carpet. As a last resort
she turns to latex, good old
industrial strength latex
which bursts predictably
at the worst possible time
just as she was wondering
how to cool down an appetite
and what are the ingredients
that leaven a life and how much loving
does it take to change a heart.

The Hat

I feel like a new man. Inside the elegant shadow
of the hat Johanna gave me I imagine I'm moving
the way a tree wears leaves, the way the earth dresses up
in night and day, how her kisses convinced me to uncover
myself and remove years of cotton and responsibility
layers of bad weather and wool, to put this Panama hat

on my vagabond head and navigate the long afternoons
and waves of sunlight. Beneath its broad and optimistic brim
I'll set my course for the high seas where life begins
under its flag I'll sail home to my only harbour, her body
buoyant on the evening calm, my cargo safe in the deep
dark hold of her heart. More than vanity or decoration

my hat is an act of devotion, a reminder of the soft touch
love requires, how vulnerable I am without tenderness.
Can you imagine an egg without a nest, pearls without a string,
this poem without a page? Could you hold a teardrop
of hot blown glass in your naked palm? Don't you see
how impossible it is to carry your heart through this world

without shade. Even the toughest skin needs protection,
the carpenter in his leather apron, the cop in his contempt.
It's more than the hole in the ozone, it's an emptiness inside
that cries out for a good headpiece, a hat made with love.
Within its circle a man may move without fear, inside
the soft crown I can lift my eyes and receive shelter

as if it were a blessing on my head or rain at the end
of a drought, a white rose rising from the fever and dust
of troubled thought. Cool, complete and unselfconscious
as any creature of feather and fur I belong
to this world, I walk through the elements
wearing this hat as lightly as the healing touch of her lips.

Arrivals

I have no fear of falling, never get alarmed
by pockets of turbulence or the weightless dip
and thump of muscle on upholstery, that quiver
as the silver arrow sinks deep in the gut
vibrato like the last high note of a Spanish song
you're gone and I already occupy the buoyant space
where memory cradles you. It's no accident

a moving staircase travels the circuit
between arrivals and departures.
I look back and imagine I'm flying
in your eyes twelve steps up
a ladder leaning on nothing more
than the spirit's promise of altitude
the heart's unscheduled flight. Wherever
the destination we'll always touch down, here
wheeling our baggage between the worlds
we're born to visit and the love that brings us home.

Five Almonds

Five almonds, half an apple and a single slice
of seven grain bread. Watch me whip up a poem
out of plain hearty food, serve love fresh
from my red clay bowl. Bite into this:
no recipe can contain a woman's secret spice
no hardwood table support her feast.
Like a fiddlehead in sweet green exclamation
her delicacy is a lifetime in the making
a dark contract with mushrooms, a musky
agreement with roots, that hint of sugar
running down the throat of every tree
as if the forest were her cupboard
and the sky a brimming bowl
where nothing goes to waste.
Step into the kitchen and breathe
the earth as it simmers, the salt
of last night's loving that brought me
to my senses, lifted me out of a bland nagging hunger
into beauty, the bird that calls all sleepers
into wakefulness. What she was in darkness
she will be in the light, opening the menu
of the morning to fill my mouth
with flavour and heap my plate with love.

Brilliance

Outside her meditation room the unruly sun
tumbles the way a child playing for time
pretends not to hear a big voice booming
out of the west and sinking to its knees
stains the windows and walls she painted
forest green. This is not the natural world

but a path to perfect the will: choosing light
choosing love, a mindful arrangement
of prayer wheels and bundles of sage
Tibetan bells and books open to invocation
where she whispers stories of the soul's
deliberation, the mark of her fingers

in clay, the lift of hair as she looks back
leaving, a gesture that wakes me like rain
draws me out of my skin into a dream
of swimming across a river, breathing deep
blue water, bodies lucid in the breaking
wave of the moment, quick as a poem

in longhand, faithful as a photograph
emerging from the darkroom of memory
in silk and brushed cotton, in fleshtones and sepia
she rises, reaching into the shadows to stop
time, to preserve the bright face of passion
from faded grey virtue and cold steel eyes.

No-one ever told me to my face
I'd be better off a saint but I heard it
hard and clear, brilliant without question
and selfless as a stone I did an anxious jig
for a pinch of affection. What was it I wanted
from those angry gods that I find inside

the room of her deepest devotion? I feel her hands
lift the stone of judgement from my back
speak my beauty as freely as the earth does
the weather, accept my fears as they fall
from these lips, the snow as it's spoken.
I know it on my skin, she doesn't require me

to repair the past or improve the man I am.
There's a ladder leaning against her wall
a window that wants my attention, that waits
for me to shine, to climb above the cloudy logic
of soap and rags, the cool abstraction of glass
to step into brilliance and offer my hands to the light.

Too Much

it's not enough
to buy you
salt shakers and parasols
sailboats in bottles
or handmade soap
that smells like the dark

wooden furniture inside
Spanish churches it's not enough
to empty dusty shelves
of dark chocolate to finger
silk and bone china
or feed the parrot in its golden cage

nothing speaks your name
or spills your secret need
though I liberate the zoo
and ransack the forest
uproot the trees
and sweet-talk the florist
though I plunge my hands
into raw earth for your pleasure

nothing requires you to love me
not the sun-baked clay and the ecstasy
of poets not the guitars and smoke
of Mexico nor the suffering
old world with its wrought iron
staircases winding through
libraries and clouds
appointments and rain

not the seduction of words
the promise to come to you
with my hands empty and strong
enough to shift the burden
of loneliness and lift the dead
weight of the material
the way I can the way I am
when you give yourself to me

Pre-Nuptial

We have these things to sort out
between us, furniture, cars, nest
eggs and air purifiers, souvenirs
of past lives, past loves. Your cool damp
basement, my unlit closet. Assumptions
about who I am and what I have
without you. And as for the wounds
and the weight of desire
they are nobody's property
the debts are paid, the account is balanced.

I'm an open book with a broken spine and hands
with a mind of their own. I've a crush on words
and a thing about cops, an aversion to cellphones
and woodticks, a sick fascination for show tunes.
I've been known to wake up singing, admit to
an unhealthy relationship with the Good Book
and all that Deuteronomy jazz, you know the tune
what Abraham tried on Isaac (not to mention Oprah).
Have I told you I'm Jewish? How I spent my youth
in bathrooms, believing I had a place in the temple
imagining I truly counted while prayers
ran through my fingers like polished wheat,
how my first love turned a fresh face and rode off
bareback into rebellion on someone else's motorcycle.

And so I put no trust in guarantees
of virtue or profit, government bonds
and church basements. I avoid those who wear
their blindness like a tragedy, their truth like a cut
flower in any old buttonhole. I can't stand dark
glasses indoors but I'm willing to put up with cats
accept the necessity of chocolate. I've grown accustomed
to my face, to eating my words, to getting it gloriously

heroically wrong. I can live with family dinners and kisses
on the cheek. I have no idea (nor do I care a fig)
what patchouli is and what its natural and un-
natural uses are but when it comes to figs, canoes
or Pacific oysters, anything faintly resembling a vulva
I'm in. I respect (and obey) lemons, it's pure poetry
how they refuse to be sweet, how sometimes
the only possible way to get clear about love is to talk
about lemons and sweaters and drywall, to
talk, to talk, to talk.

Let me tell you about my shelf
of faded towels and left wing sympathies
my considerable dental experience
when I sat back frozen while spring blew by
how I still say *ah* to the good life, deep kisses
and coherent conversation, whole grains
and heartsmart cuisine. Though we have a history
I bear no grudge against tofu.
When it comes to red meat I'm your man.
But I'm no saint.

I get pissed off at the hegemony
of television, American foreign policy
line-ups at the florist, prostate
examinations, anything pushy
or fraught with an unwarranted belief
in its own transcendence. I shy away
from folks who toss words like *hegemony*
fraught and *transcendence* into the *soup*
du jour. Don't get me started on the butchers
of free speech and the stained knickers
of the fifth estate. I'm old enough to believe
in social justice, universal healthcare
the cultivation of marijuana on the rooftop
of every personal care home. I have a dream:

I want the homeless to sleep
in the same warmth and comfort we keep
our dollars. Give the poor PIN numbers, access
to *feng shui* and Broadway musicals, the opportunity
to climb the odd blonde mountain with a flock
of happy Germans in leather. I'll confess
I'm turned on by singing nuns, own up to the murder
of one unfaithful folding chair and the occasional umbrella.

Now that I'm yours what I want from you
I cannot keep. Commitment is as difficult
as poetry. It's more than possession or how
the parts fit together, more than the way we touch
it's how we hold ourselves. Love is no adhesive
for broken vessels, it's that light burning between two
worlds where I am finally seen in full disclosure,
it's the border between flesh and spirit
where there's nothing left to hide.

What It Takes (to bury the hatchet)

Forgive me. It's not the moon
but your body melting
the fine animal gallops
a luminous breast groomed

in perfumed silk
and midnight whispers
my hand *sotto voce*
in the hollow of your back

waltzing through champagne
and cleavage a one and a two
a me and a you
down the polished staircase

into a dream. Didn't we pay
the orchestra to play all night
didn't we beg
the music never to stop?

The risk of cardiac arrest
spikes 49% Monday morning
and ain't that a killer
between bed and business

the wheel stops
the golden hour shatters
opaque as bone china
the heart keeps time

heaving its cargo of blood
as if it were the one responsible
while the madcap brain trumpets
the brass annunciation

new gods, new obligations
to rise up and ride
into the jaws of the morning
and raise the vascular cavalry

from the languid otherworld
of sleep. Good luck Crazy Horse.
Let the old pump thunder
over lipstick and tissue

dried flowers and reminders
of a time when love required
no uniform but the tree of bone
and being (imagine the pleasure

of naming each sensation)
the temporal blossoming
of bodies, the sweetness
that bursts above the earth

bends the branches of the self
toward the sun. Armour and all
I am a leaf on the stem of memory
I am the fire your loving lights

Journeyman

It used to be I was the poet's lone apprentice, her secret
reader, the middle finger that nudged her pen forward
night and day. Used to be she had me running

errands through the lyrical streets. That was me whistling
around the corner flogging the explicit propositions
of her fruit, the ecstasy of furniture she kept hidden

beyond the reach of ordinary lamps. Once she was the needle
I her thread and beneath the silver thimble I heard a bell
inside the cathedral of her crushed felt fedora

I gave away ashes and pomegranates, beckoned
to bartenders and statues through the screen
of the confessional, in her name I'd walk around

talking to the trees. That's all behind me, now the sorrow
of falling leaves is my own and the willow has grown heavy
with answers, I hear voices everywhere but I am careful

to beg her intercession only for simple gifts, easy births
a clean death, my children's health restored.
I am realistic about probable outcomes, fully aware

of the risks in talking to trees, or anyone else. I expect nothing
and in return, nothing happens. *Selah*. Call it illusion
how the earth meets my eye when I bend low, asking

after her health in the maestro's latin tongue *Felicitame
abuelita* Grandmother wish me well *estoy libre
contento* I am satisfied and free *e ya basta*

already I have enough

Solstice 2005

Whatever else may happen
on this day when the sun stops
to kiss our eccentric planet

my lips declare a revolution, here
where it's too hot to embrace
where the shades come down

to attend the birth of a season
and all things being equal
my plum tree blossoms

in your name and I imagine fruit
all winter long eating out of the jar
I turn the bright tin lid to think

of you the dark jagged moon
in dusty spoonfuls of shadow
and sweetness preserved I confess

in the distillation of memory
and the imperfect will that absorbs my losses
in the roundness of this bowl

come high summer I will be water I will
know your tongue your teeth your thirst
to follow the sun and the gods

forgetful of speech will see themselves
bending like trees to breathe the earth
through darkness and through light.

Smudge

Without love how would I be here
to see this day dying how would I notice
the golden light anointing airborne
wings, the holy outcry of ice
letting go and birds as they soar
and descend, returning to touch
the open water of ancestral lakes, the nests
that hold their deep blue history and perfect
oval future. Once again I am here, in time
for the arrival of eagles and untold geese
more ducks than I can name: *Mallards* and *Teal*
Bufflehead and *Goldeneye*, each one
recognizing their home in creation, gifted
to read the opinion of the wind and call out
the complete story of up and down. Myself
I don't need to know why they fly or who
dictates the revolution of heaven and earth
it's enough to see the season turn, to hear
the hum of generation and witness how they govern
the green shifting territory between water and sand.
This country where I am always a guest, walking
along the edge, welcomed and cleansed
in the smudge of the setting sun.

Coming to my Senses
the third Johanna poem

I was the only one who could stop
myself, loving. I was rolling
along and growing old
as I've told you so many times
before I was shrinking inside
my skin, so transparent
with want that I pulled shut
the window, I was a glass
wall. That was me, my lips
mashed grotesque against the triple
pane, that was my breath
obliterating the view.
I was stretched. I was poisoned.
And then I forgave myself.

No. That's not entirely true
I was given permission to step through
the fear and ceaseless chatter and call out
in a voice I'd never used before
to breathe deep and walk freely
whatever place on earth I choose
to set my foot. Permission to know
my skin the way the apple does
coming into fullness at the end
of the season. Now I can tell you
about the sweetness under the sun
declare the ripe round truth
that I'm beginning to speak with tenderness
I'm learning to close with love.